Children learn to read by reading, but they need help to begin with.

When you have read the story on the left-hand pages aloud to the child, go back to the beginning of the book and look at the pictures together.

Encourage children to read the sentences under the pictures. If they don't know a word, give them a chance to 'guess' what it is from the illustrations, before telling them.

There are more suggestions for helping children to learn to read in the *Parent/Teacher* booklet.

British Library Cataloguing in Publication Data

McCullagh, Sheila K.
   The magic dust.—(Puddle Lane series; stage 3/8).
   1. Readers—*1950-*
   I. Title   II. Dillow, John   III. Series
   428.6   PE1119
   ISBN 0-7214-1073-1

First edition

Published by Ladybird Books Ltd Loughborough Leicestershire UK
Ladybird Books Inc Lewiston Maine 04240 USA

© Text and layout SHEILA McCULLAGH MCMLXXXVIII
© In publication LADYBIRD BOOKS LTD MCMLXXXVIII

Printed in England

The magic dust

written by SHEILA McCULLAGH
illustrated by JOHN DILLOW

This book belongs to:

BARRY

Ladybird Books

Chestnut Mouse was out in Puddle Lane,
looking for something to eat,
when it suddenly began to rain.
There was no warning.
The rain poured down,
streaming off the roofs of the houses
in a dozen little waterfalls.
Chestnut saw a broken flower pot
by Mr Puffle's front door.
He ran over to it and crept inside,
to wait until the rain was over.

It was raining in Puddle Lane.
Chestnut crept into a flower pot.

He heard the gates of the Magician's
garden bang to. He looked out, and saw
the Gruffle coming down the lane.
The Gruffle was a monster.
He was always gruff and grumpy,
but he hated rain.
He was looking very angry
as he stamped down the lane,
breathing out little puffs of fire and smoke.
But Chestnut wasn't frightened, because
he knew the Gruffle was afraid of mice.

Chestnut looked out
of the flower pot.
He saw the Gruffle in Puddle Lane.

The rain stopped and the sun came out.
Chestnut was just going to run out
into the lane, when he saw Mr Puffle.
He hid at the back of the flower pot.
Suddenly, there was a great CRASH!
There was a roar from the Gruffle,
and the sound of running feet.
Chestnut peeped out of the flower pot.
Mr Puffle was staggering to his front door,
and the Gruffle was standing in the lane,
roaring, with potatoes lying all around him.
As Chestnut watched, a toy mouse
landed in the lane beside the Gruffle.
The Gruffle roared again, and vanished.

Chestnut saw the Gruffle
standing in the lane.
The Gruffle roared.

9

Chestnut looked up.

Hari was looking out of an upstairs window.

As Chestnut watched, he disappeared inside.

A few moments later,

Hari came out into the lane with Gita.

They picked up the toy mouse.

Then they picked up the potatoes,

put them in a sack, and left them

inside Mr Puffle's front door.

They went inside their own house again.

Chestnut didn't wait any longer.

He ran off up Puddle Lane

as fast as he could run.

He was very excited.

Hari and Gita went inside.
Chestnut ran off up Puddle Lane
as fast as he could run.

The Wideawake Mice were all at home,
when Chestnut came rushing down
the mousehole.
"I've seen a mouse!" he cried,
falling over himself with excitement.
"I've seen a toy mouse.
It was dressed just the way you are.
It must be a Wideawake Mouse!"

"Where was it?" asked Aunt Jane.

"In one of the houses in Puddle Lane.
That boy, Hari, dropped it in the lane,
but he took it back into the house."

"I've seen a mouse!"
cried Chestnut.
"I've seen a toy mouse.
It must be a Wideawake Mouse."

"It must be Father or Mother!"
cried Miranda.
"Someone came into the toyshop, and
bought them, before we came alive.
We must go and find them."

"Wait a bit," said Grandfather Mouse.
"We've got to think carefully.
We only came alive because the Magician
spilt some magic dust over us.
We must try and get some magic dust,
so that they can come alive, too."

"I don't see how we can ever
get magic dust," said Uncle Maximus.
"We must ask the Magician for some,"
said Grandmother Mouse.

"We must get some magic dust,"
said Grandfather Mouse.
"We must ask the Magician
for some," said Grandmother Mouse.

"We'll have to wait till it's dark,"
said Chestnut. "It's not very safe,
running about the garden in the daytime.
We'll go and see the Magician tonight."

"The mouseholes in the Magician's house
aren't as big as I should like them to be,"
said Grandfather Mouse.
"I'll go and get the magic dust,"
said Chestnut.
"I'll go with you," said Jeremy.
"So will I," said Miranda.
"I wish I could go with you,"
said Aunt Jane. "But it's no good.
I can't use my foot yet."
(Aunt Jane had got a thorn
in her back paw, and it was
very painful.)
She gave Chestnut a little sack,
for the magic dust.

"I will go and get the magic dust,"
said Chestnut.
"I will go with you," said Jeremy.
"So will I," said Miranda.

As soon as it was dark,
the three little mice ran off
through the Magician's garden,
and through a hole under the door
into the hall of the big house.
"This way!" squeaked Chestnut.
They ran up the stairs to the landing.
Chestnut found the mousehole leading up
through the walls of the old house
to the Magician's room, and
they all scrambled up through it
as fast as they could.

Chestnut found the mousehole
that led to the Magician's room.

They came out into the Magician's room.
There was no one there.
The cauldron was bubbling on the fire,
and the firelight shone on the big chair.
"I wonder where he is?" whispered Jeremy.

"I don't know," said Chestnut.
"I thought he'd be here."

"We shall have to find the magic dust
by ourselves," said Miranda.
"I'm sure the Magician would give us some,
if he were here."

The Magician was not in his room.
"We must find the magic dust,"
said Miranda.

The little mice scampered all over the room,
looking for the silver box of magic dust.
Chestnut and Jeremy explored the table,
but the box wasn't there.
Miranda climbed all over the big chair,
and then ran up onto the mantelpiece.
She saw the little dragon sitting there,
and for a moment she was frightened.
But then she remembered that
the little dragon had turned into stone.
Something was shining on the other side
of the dragon.
Miranda climbed over his tail —
and saw the silver box!
"It's here!" she cried. "It's here!"

Miranda saw the little dragon.
She climbed over the dragon's tail,
and saw the silver box!

Chestnut and Jeremy ran up the wall,
and along the mantelpiece to join her.
"That's it!" said Jeremy. "That's the box
the Magician had in Mr Wideawake's shop."

"How does it open?" asked Chestnut.

"There's a lid," said Jeremy.
"We'll have to push the box over,
and pull off the lid."
They all stood up on their back feet,
and pushed.
The box fell over. The lid fell off.
Some magic dust spilled out.

The mice stood up
on their back feet, and pushed.
The box fell over.

"Put some magic dust in Aunt Jane's sack,"
said Miranda.
They were so busy pushing the dust
into the sack with their front paws,
that they didn't notice that some of it
had floated up into the air
and settled on the little dragon.

The mice pushed the magic dust
into the sack.
Some of the dust
fell on the little dragon.

"The sack's full," said Jeremy.

"Come on," said Chestnut. "I'll carry it.
Let's go back to the hollow tree."
They ran down the wall to the floor,
and back towards the mousehole.

"Let's go back," said Chestnut.
They ran down the wall, and
back to the mousehole.

At that moment, the moon
came out from behind a cloud,
and shone into the Magician's room.
A long finger of moonlight
touched the little dragon.
The dragon's eyes opened.

The moon shone
on the little dragon.
The dragon's eyes opened.

The next moment, the little dragon
was hurtling down through the air
towards the mice.
Chestnut had just pulled the sack
into the mousehole.
Jeremy and Miranda gave
one startled look at the little dragon,
and dived into the hole after him.

Jeremy and Miranda
saw the dragon.
They dived into the hole.

"Quick!" cried Miranda. "Quick, Chestnut!
The little dragon's come alive again!"
Chestnut pulled the sack of magic dust
into a corner in the hole.
Jeremy and Miranda leapt forwards,
and fell on top of him.
They were just in time.
A long flame shot down into the hole,
but it couldn't reach them.
They heard the little dragon hiss with rage,
and then he was gone.

Chestnut pulled the sack
into a corner.
Jeremy and Miranda
fell on top of him.

The little dragon flew up into the air.
He was just going to set the room on fire,
when he heard the Magician coming.
He didn't wait.
He flew to the open window,
and out into the darkness,
and away over the roofs
of the houses in Candletown.

The little dragon flew away,
out of the window, and
over the roofs of the houses.

Chestnut poked his head through the hole
in the Magician's front door.
He looked out into the garden, and listened.
"The dragon's gone," he whispered.
"Come on."
The three little mice crept out
into the Magician's garden.
The moon was shining down,
and they hid in the dark shadows.

The three little mice crept out
into the Magician's garden.

Grandfather Mouse and Aunt Jane
were waiting for them by the hollow tree.
"Did you get the dust?" asked Grandfather.

"Yes," said Jeremy. "But some of it fell
on the little dragon. He came alive.
He isn't stone any longer."

"We shall have to look out for him,"
said Aunt Jane. "But you're safely back.
And you've got the magic dust.
That's the most important thing."

"Can we go and find Father and
Mother now?" asked Miranda.

"It's too late tonight," said Grandfather.
"We'll go tomorrow, as soon as it's dark."
They all went down into the hole
under the hollow tree.

Grandfather Mouse and
Aunt Jane were outside
the hollow tree.

When the Magician went into his room,
he smelt smoke.
He looked for the little dragon –
but the little dragon had gone.
The box of magic dust was on its side,
and some of the dust lay on the
mantelpiece, where the dragon had been.
The Magician shook his head.
"Now there'll be trouble," he said.
"I wonder where that little dragon
has got to?"

The Magician looked for
the little dragon,
but the little dragon had gone.

If you would like to know what happened next, read:

Stage 3

If you have not read about the Wideawake Mice before, you can find the story of how they came alive and more stories about their adventures in:

Stage 1

Stage 2

*from
Tom Cat
and the
Wideawake Mice*

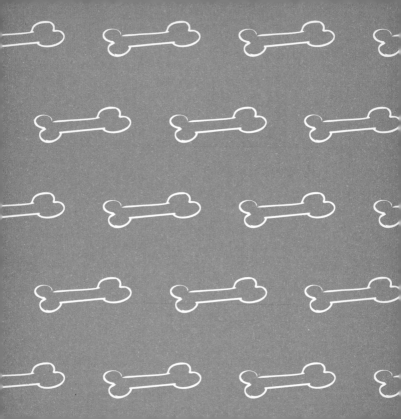

You Know You're a
Dog Lover
When...

Ben Fraser

Illustrations by Roger Penwill

summersdale

YOU KNOW YOU'RE A DOG LOVER WHEN…

Summersdale Publishers Ltd
46 West Street
Chichester
West Sussex
PO19 1RP
UK

www.summersdale.com

Printed and bound in China

ISBN: 978-1-84953-092-7

Substantial discounts on bulk quantities of Summersdale books are available to corporations, professional associations and other organisations. For details contact Summersdale Publishers by telephone: +44 (0) 1243 771107, fax: +44 (0) 1243 786300 or email: nicky@summersdale.com.

To..

From..

The dog has his own place at the dining table so he can eat with the family.

Your mobile ringtone is 'Who Let the Dogs Out?'

You always coordinate your outfit to match your mutt's – who said dog collars aren't in?

You've been on so many long-distance walkies that your dog rivals Bear Grylls in tackling extreme outdoor conditions.

You don't mind that your dog
has more friends than you
on Facebook.

Your prized possession is your novelty telephone: a dog and bone, of course!

You spend hours searching the website Muttmatcher.com to locate your perfect canine companion.

Your friend goes to borrow some shampoo from your bathroom and is confused to find that all the bottles read 'for a rich, glossy coat'.

You own more tennis balls
than Andy Murray.

You bribe the judges at Crufts so you
can take their front row seats and be
closest to the action.

You believe that fine art has its place, but insist that there's nothing finer than a picture of a bulldog and his pals playing pool.

You spend hours training for
dog agility competitions –
even on your pooch's day off.

Your friend mentions someone who's 'a
real bitch' and you think she sounds
like an ideal playmate for your
new pooch.

The most expensive things in your house are the 2,000-count Egyptian cotton sheets on which your dog sleeps.

You save all of your dog's fur –
to knit into a stylish jumper.

You spend hours grooming your beloved bow-wow – you occasionally run a comb through your own hair, but you and your dog both know who the looker is.

You refuse to wear patterned clothes unless they are houndstooth – well, except for your pyjamas with cute little bones on.

You do your bit for dog–human equality by holding a charity dogsled race, where the owners pull huskies on sleds through the snow.

You have the Kennel Club
down as your emergency
contact number.

You have taken on enough
rescue dogs to become a
serious rival to Battersea
Dogs & Cats Home.

You write to the council demanding
that they install a dog loo with
separate cubicles in your local park –
after all, a dog has his dignity
to consider.

You start a canine-themed CD collection for your dog, which includes David Bowie's *Diamond Dogs*, Ozzy Osbourne's *Bark at the Moon* and everything by Wolfmother.

You can trace your dog's family
tree further back than
your own.

You realise you are not so much the
dog whisperer as the dog yodeller,
after your prized Alsatian runs amok
in the park.

You have premium pet insurance which covers your dog for the emotional strain of excessive moulting.

Your neighbours are alarmed
at the amount of bones in your
back garden and alert
the police.

You arrive on holiday and immediately call your dogsitter and have them put Fido on the phone so you can tell him just how much 'Mummy' and 'Daddy' are missing him.

You have subscriptions to all the must-have monthlies – *Dog World, Puppy Dog Tales* and, of course, *Chihuahua Connection* magazine.

You have over two decades'
worth of 'autographs' from the
Blue Peter dogs.

Your DVD collection consists exclusively
of movies in which dogs share star
billing – Tom Hanks and a slobbering
French Mastiff, what's not to like?!

You perch on the arm of your sofa instead of getting your dog to move... it just looks too cute and comfortable.

You watched so much *Lassie* growing up that if you hear a Collie barking you immediately run to the local police station to report a suspected 'boy down a well' scenario.

You have an obedience ring –
and make family members sit
in it.

Your dog has its own travel
arrangements in first class, as well as
its own platinum frequent flyer
club card.

Family Christmas cards feature
only the four-legged family members
wearing Santa hats and little
black booties.

You always request 'Roll Over, Beethoven' by Chuck Berry at discos, and proceed to imitate a St Bernard doing just that in the middle of the dance floor.

Over half your garden is taken up by the luxury kennel you built for your star canine – complete with bone-shaped paddling pool.

You spend so much money on organic dog food the company makes you its chief shareholder.

You spend so much money on organic
dog food the company makes you its
chief shareholder.

Your friends think you've turned into a West Coast gangster since you've started using the phrase "Sup, dawg?" on a regular basis.

You serenade your dog at dinnertime every night, à la *Lady and the Tramp*.

Your partner buys you
personalised dog tags for
Valentine's Day.

You're so handy with your pooper scooper that you've earned the nickname 'The Va·poo·riser'.

You firmly believe that cats are
actually a lesser form of canine which,
thanks to their haughty nature, failed
to evolve any further.

You know the name of every dog you pass on the canal during walkies, but fail to recognise any of their owners.

Your friends refuse to get in your car as they know they will come out looking like a yeti from the build-up of Rex's hair in the back.

You love long walks along the beach
and sharing an ice cream while
watching the sun go down – with your
perfect pooch, obviously.

You refer to your closest friends as your 'pack'.

You go shopping for a special
birthday outfit... for your dog.

Your colleagues ask about your nearest and dearest and you immediately show them the framed photos of Sir Fluffy Barkington III featured in pride of place on your desk.

You become fascinated with
astronomy after you discover
the Dog Star.

You splash out on a Pampered Paws spa day for your dog on its birthday.

You always cause trouble,
because you just can't let
sleeping dogs lie.

Your neighbours refuse to speak to you after seeing the way you 'marked your territory' on either side of your garden.

You spend the whole day cuddling the dog whenever you are hungover, but feel the 'hair of the dog' is not quite as effective as people make out.

You devote your free time to finding more interesting ways to present your dog's dinner, although kibble en croûte didn't go down too well last time.

One of your favourite pastimes is recreating famous film scenes with your canine co-star.

You use your Nicky Clarke
style album to create fabulous
new looks for your pooch.

You have a habit of absently patting your children on the head.

Canine yoga is your new favourite hobby, which includes such positions as 'The Ear Scratch' and 'Watering the Lamppost'.

You haven't read a letter or newspaper
in the past decade which hasn't been
well ventilated with teeth marks.

You are frequently seen carrying your precious pup around in a baby sling, making comments like 'Who's Mummy's little precious?' in a mushy voice.

You own every Spaniel-themed ceramic plate known to man, along with Spaniel-themed cushion covers, mugs, key rings and a personalised 'I Love Spaniels' T-shirt.

You start telling people that
your bark is worse than
your bite.

Someone says they think you look fetching and you immediately go and retrieve the nearest stick.

You are disappointed to discover that, aside from the star's shaggy haircut, *Dog the Bounty Hunter* has very little to do with canines or their owners.

After staring into your dog's eyes for hours on end you are beginning to believe you have a telepathic link with your pooch.

You've been banned from group sports because you like to play 'ruff'.

You take your pooch to the
park so often you know
exactly what it is to be
'dog tired'.

You refer to those extra few pounds you've been carrying for years as 'puppy fat' – you must give up those doggy treats!

Your favourite pub is the Dog and Duck.

You hold classes for water-shy canines: 'The Art of Doggy-paddling'.

You have an inexplicable dislike for the postman and can't resist growling if you see him pass by.

Have you enjoyed this book?
If so, why not write a review
on your favourite website?

Thanks very much for buying
this Summersdale book.

www.summersdale.com

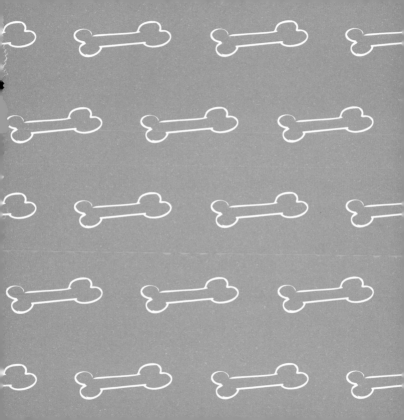

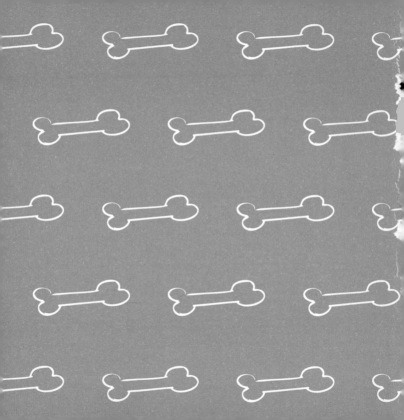